INFANCY GOSPEL OF THOMAS

(*Thomas the Israelite Philosopher's Account of the Infancy of the Lord.*)

Edited by

JAMES ORR

LONDON: J.M. DENT & CO.: 1903
PHILADELPHIA: J.B. LIPPINCOTT CO.

Please See The Back Page For More Great Titles
Available Through CrossReach Publications.
And If You Enjoyed This Book Please Consider Leaving A
Review On Amazon. That Helps Us Out A Lot. Thanks.

CrossReach
Publications
Available In Paperback And eBook Editions
© 2016 CrossReach Publications
All Rights Reserved, Including The Right To Reproduce
This Book Or Portions Thereof In Any Form Whatever.

Introduction

The Canonical Gospels. As far back as we can trace them the four Gospels known as Canonical hold a place of honour and authority peculiar to themselves. Irenæus of Gaul (*circa* A.D. 175) recognises four, and only four, Gospels as the 'pillars' that uphold the Church (*Adv. Haer.* iii. 8). Origen, in the beginning of the next century (A.D. 220), speaks of them as 'the four Gospels which alone are uncontroverted in the Church of God spread under heaven' (Euseb., *H. E.* vi. 25). Justin Martyr, in the middle of the second century, narrates that the 'Memoirs of the Apostles,' which are called Gospels, were read every Sunday in the assemblies of the Christians (*Apol.* 66, 67). That these Gospels were those we now possess we can tell, not only from Justin's description of them, and allusions to their contents (*cp.* Sanday's *Gospels in Second Century*, chap. iv.), but from the harmony made of them by his disciple Tatian in his *Diatessaron* (now recovered in Arabic translations). Our four Gospels, and these only, stand at the head of the ancient Syriac (*Peshitta*), the Latin and the Egyptian versions (*cp.* Westcott and Hort), and of the old list known as the Canon of Muratori (*circa* A.D. 180). Within the Church, in short, our four Gospels, attributed by second-century

The Infancy Gospel of Thomas

writers to their present authors, had never any rivals.

Apocryphal Writings. It stands very differently, as respects origin, character and reception, with the Gospels, Acts and Apocalpyses known as 'Apocryphal.' These began to be produced (so far as known) in the second century, mostly in Ebionitic and Gnostic circles, and, with few exceptions, were repudiated and condemned by the Church. Only later, and in modified and expurgated forms, did their stories pass into the general Catholic tradition. The second century seems to have been a perfect hot-bed for the production of this class of writings. The heretical *Gospel of the Egyptians* is already quoted in 2 Clement (*circa* A.D. 140). Irenæus speaks of the sect of the Marcosians as adducing 'an unspeakable number of apocryphal and spurious writings, which they themselves had forged, to bewilder the minds of the foolish,' and instances the story, found in the *Gospel of Thomas*, of Jesus confounding the schoolmaster who sought to teach Him His letters (*Adv. Haer.* i. 20). Later tradition attributed the composition of many of the apocryphal writings (*Pseudo-Matthew*, Acts of Apostles) to a mythical Leucius, a disciple of the Apostles (*cp.* art. 'Leucius,' *Dict. of Christ.*

Biog.). Eusebius gives a list of spurious and disputed books: 'That we may have it in our power to know both these books (the canonical) and those that are adduced by the heretics under the name of the Apostles, such, viz., as compose the Gospels of Peter, of Thomas, and of Matthew, and certain others beside these, or such as contain the Acts of Andrew and John, and of the other Apostles, of which no one of those writers in the ecclesiastical succession has condescended to make any mention in his works; and, indeed, the character of the style itself is very different from that of the Apostles, and the sentiments, and the purport of those things that are advanced in them, deviating as far as possible from sound orthodoxy, evidently proves they are the fictions of heretical men; whence they are not only to be ranked among the spurious writings, but are to be rejected as altogether absurd and impious' (*H. E.* iii. 25). Only a small part of this extensive literature remains to us, and in no case in its original form, but solely in later, and often much-altered recensions.

Authorities. The apocryphal literature is a study by itself, with the intricate details of which only specialists are competent to deal. Great attention has been bestowed on the collecting, editing and collating of such codices of Gospels,

The Infancy Gospel of Thomas

Acts, and other writings as were formerly known, or have more recently been discovered. The most important of the older collections was that of Fabricius (*Codex Apocryphus*, 1719). The collections and prolegomena of Thilo (1832) and Tischendorf (*Acts*, 1851; *Gospels*, 1853; *Apocalypses*, 1856) are of special value; much, however, has been done since their time. The articles by Lipsius in the *Dict. of Christ. Biog.* on 'Acts of the Apostles (Apocryphal)' and 'Gospels (Apocryphal)', are, like the author's learned German work (2 vols., 1883) on the former subject, masterly in their discussions of the relations of the documents. Valuable light was thrown on the Syriac versions of the *Protevangelium of James*, the *Gospel of Thomas*, and the *Transitus Mariæ* (Passing of Mary), by the texts and fragments edited and translated by Dr. W. Wright in the *Journal of Sacred Literature* (January and April 1865), and his *Contributions to the Apocryphal Literature of the New Testament* (1865), and *Apocryphal Acts of the Apostles* (1871). In 1902 Mrs. Agnes Smith Lewis edited, with translations and other illustrative matter, new Syriac texts of the *Protevangelium* and *Transitus Mariæ*, obtained from a palimpsest she was fortunate enough to purchase at Suez in July 1895 (*Studia Sinaitica*, No. XI. 1902). An interesting fragment of the lost *Gospel of Peter* (second century) was discovered, with other MSS., at Akhmim, in Upper Egypt, in 1886, and was published in 1892. A translation of the Apocryphal Gospels was published in 1874 by Mr. B. H. Cowper, on the basis of Tischendorf's edition; and Vol. XVI. of Messrs. T. & T. Clark's *Ante-Nicene Library* is devoted to translations by Mr. A. Walker of 'Apocryphal Gospels, Acts and Revelations.' An 'Additional Volume' of the *Library* (1897) contains translations of works more recently discovered Lectures XI. and XIX. of Dr. Salmon's *Introduction to the New Testament*, on 'Apocryphal and Heretical Gospels' and 'Apocryphal Acts of the Apostles,' may profitably be consulted. Hone's catch-penny *Apocryphal New Testament* (1820) is critically worthless.

Character of Apocryphal Gospels. Of the purely heretical Gospels most have perished (for an account of some of the Gnostic ones, *see* Baring-Gould's *Lost and Hostile Gospels* (1874), and Lipsius, as above). But apart from doctrinal reasons, sufficient motive always existed in persons of lax tendency to pander to the principle of curiosity and love of the marvellous in human nature by inventions of narratives on subjects on which the genuine Gospels were silent. An existing narrative, or traditions of sayings and doings of Jesus, might be, and frequently were, manipulated, recast, or embellished; but the grand opportunity came when the Gospels said nothing at all. Here was a space which imagination could fill up at pleasure. The stories might be puerile, demoralising, ridiculous to the last degree, but if they were only circumstantial and marvellous enough, and were backed up by names of Apostles, or others of repute, the narrator could always rely on finding readers greedy to receive them. This is precisely what happened with the Apocryphal Gospels. There are differences in degree of puerility and extravagance; but Bishop Ellicott did not exaggerate when he said of the spurious Gospels as a whole (and the same remarks apply as a rule to the Acts): 'Their real demerits, their mendacities, their absurdities, their coarseness, the barbarities of their style and the inconsequence of their narratives, have never been excused or condoned. It would be hard to find any competent writer, in any age of the Church, who has been beguiled into saying anything civil or commendatory' ('On the Apocryphal Gospels,' *Cambridge Essays*, 1856, p. 153). It is to be remembered, on the other hand, that the stories in these Gospels did ultimately very deeply influence Catholic tradition.

Cycles of Narration. The stories in the Apocryphal Gospels will be found on examination to resolve themselves mainly into three groups, or to form three chief cycles, corresponding to those parts of the evangelical narrative where curiosity is most excited, and receives least satisfaction. These cycles relate (1) to the previous history of the parents of Jesus, especially of Mary, and to the Nativity; (2) to the boyhood of Jesus from His childhood to His twelfth year; and (3) to the passion of Jesus, and the interval between His death and Resurrection.

A few words may be said on the cycles generally before passing to the special introduction.

1. Cycle on the Parents of Jesus and on the Nativity. Joseph and Mary are somewhat abruptly introduced in the genuine Gospels, while a long preliminary history is given in Luke of Zacharias and Elizabeth, the parents of John the Baptist. This was plainly something to be remedied, and the oldest cycle of stories, apparently without a scintilla of real tradition behind them, relate to the parentage and birth of the Virgin Mary, the wonderful circumstances of her early life, her betrothal to Joseph, the Annunciation, and the events of the Nativity. The stories grow in detail and in wonderful character as they advance from the *Protevangelium of James* (the oldest), through the *Gospel of Pseudo-Matthew*, to a third piece, *The Nativity of Mary*. But the main outlines of the narrative are early fixed. They include such features as the following:—How Mary's parents, Joachim and Anna, were rich, but childless; Joachim's distress at being repulsed from the Temple because he had no seed; his flight and fasting, and the grief of Anna; the angelic promise to the godly pair; the birth of Mary, and her dedication to God; the marvellous incidents of her infancy; how she lived with other virgins at the Temple from her third to her twelfth (or fourteenth) year, behaving astonishingly, and being fed by angels; how an aged guardian of her virginity was sought for, and by a Divine sign was found in Joseph, to whom, accordingly, she was betrothed; the Annunciation to Mary; Joseph's concern at her condition; the trial of Joseph and Mary by the water of jealousy at the Temple; the journey to Bethlehem, and birth of Jesus in a cave outside the city; the marvels attending the Nativity, etc. In the later versions of the legend the growing exaltation of Mary is very apparent. New stories arise also of the death of Joseph, and of the passing of the soul of Mary, and assumption of her body (*Transitus Mariæ*). Of the latter type of story one specimen is given.

2. The Boyhood of Jesus. The entire silence of the Gospel history on the early life of Jesus naturally afforded scope for invention, and the legend-mongers of the second and later centuries did not miss their opportunity. The blank in the narrative of the childhood and youth of Jesus was early filled up with an abundance of prodigies of the crudest and most puerile kind. The parent of this class of Gospel, or rather the earliest form of it, was the so-called *Gospel of Thomas*, which had its successors in the *Gospel of Pseudo-Matthew*, and, still later, in the wildly-extravagant *Arabic Gospel of the Infancy*. The absurdity of the sayings and doings attributed to the boy Jesus in this cycle of stories is only equalled by their grotesque incongruity with His real character. The single effect of placing them alongside the narratives of the genuine Gospels must be, as Dr. Westcott has said, to impress the reader with the sense of 'complete contrast.' Time, place, propriety, even ordinary consistency, are recklessly disregarded. Jesus has and exercises from His cradle all Divine powers—is omniscient, omnipotent, etc.—yet plays with the children in the street, and amuses Himself by making pools of water and moulding clay sparrows. When challenged for breaking the Sabbath, He claps His hands and His sparrows fly away. He is the terror of the places in which

The Infancy Gospel of Thomas

He resides. If boy or man offends, or contradicts Him, He smites the offender dead, or otherwise avenges Himself. He confounds His teachers, and instructs them in the mysteries of the Hebrew letters. When His pitcher breaks, He carries home the water in His lap. He aids Joseph in his carpentry by lengthening or shortening the pieces of wood at pleasure. The *Gospel of Pseudo-Matthew* gives a special series of miracles wrought by Jesus as a child in Egypt (chaps. xvii. to xxv. These chapters only are included in this volume). The *Arabic Gospel of the Infancy* gives the rein to fancy in stories of marvels and transformations, which, in their bizarre extravagance, remind of nothing so much as of the *Arabian Nights*.

3. Cycle of Pilate and Nicodemus. The evangelists give full narratives of the events of the betrayal, trial, Crucifixion, and Resurrection of Jesus. The excuse of silence, therefore, cannot be pleaded here. The apocryphal narrators, however, saw room for embellishment, expansion, and sometimes modification. Later, apparently within the Catholic Church itself, they produced a series of fictitious writings, bearing on the parts taken by Pilate, Nicodemus, Joseph of Arimathea and others, in these scenes of the Saviour's suffering and triumph. First came a number of alleged letters and reports from Pilate, doubtful in date and origin, but none in their present form early. Then appeared in varying recensions the so-called *Acts of Pilate* or *Gospel of Nicodemus*, which certainly is not older than the fourth, and is possibly as late as the fifth, century. The sobriety of the Gospel histories did not satisfy the taste of these enterprising compilers. Jesus was not made to appear sufficiently Divine in his trial before the Roman procurators; Pilate's sympathy with Jesus was not sufficiently accentuated; the testimony to Christ's innocence was not thrown into bold enough relief. All this was now amended. The altercation between Pilate and Christ's accusers assumes a lengthened and highly dramatic form; Pilate avows himself unequivocally on Christ's side; the Saviour has miraculous attestation of His dignity, *e.g.*, in the Roman standards bowing down to Him as He passes with honour into the judgment hall; the persons whose healings are narrated in the Gospels—the impotent man of John 5, the woman with the issue of blood, Bartimæus, those from whom demons had been expelled, step forward and bear witness to His power. The same kind of elaboration appears in the parts taken in the history by Nicodemus and Joseph; the whole culminating in the testimony before the

Sanhedrim by eye-witnesses to the Ascension of Jesus, on receiving which Annas, Caiaphas and the Rabbis believe! A second part of the Gospel (later in origin, and not included in this selection) recounts from the lips of the two sons of Symeon, raised from the dead, the triumphs of Jesus in Hades, during the interval between His death and Resurrection.

Apocryphal Acts of the Apostles. The same motives which led to the composition of Apocryphal Gospels naturally led to the production of a multitude of spurious Acts of Apostles. These profess to narrate the journeyings, doings and teachings of the Apostles of Christ (Peter, Thomas, Andrew, Thaddæus, Matthew, etc.) after their dispersion from Jerusalem. The groundwork of several of the Acts belongs to the second century, though, in their present form, most are Catholic recastings of much later date. The *Acts of Peter and Paul*, which relate the conflicts of these Apostles with Simon Magus are of this character (in their present form probably from fourth or fifth century). The *Acts of Thomas* still bear on them the clear imprint of the Gnosticism in which they originated (second or third century). Old 'Journeyings of Peter' are wrought up in the Ebionitic *Clementine* writings (second century).

The oldest and freshest extant specimen of this class of literature is the *Acts of Paul and Thecla*, on which *see* below. The apocryphal 'Apocalypses,' of which there were a great many (of Paul, Peter, John, etc.), must here be left unnoticed. A fragment of the *Apocalypse of Peter* was discovered with the *Gospel of Peter* at Akhmim in 1886, and was published in 1902.

Something may now be said by way of more special introduction to the apocryphal work included in this volume.

The Infancy Gospel of Thomas. This Gospel gives the account of the sayings and doings, but specially of the miracles, of Jesus in His boyhood up to His twelfth year. The reference to one of the stories in Irenæus (above, p. vi.), shows that the work originated in Gnostic circles, and was in use in substance in the second half of the second century. It is cited by Origen (*Hom.* i. *in Luc.*), and after him frequently by Fathers of the Church. We do not, however, possess the Gospel in its original form, but only in much later Catholic recasts—two of them Greek, one Latin, and one Syriac. Of the first and longer Greek version (that adopted in this volume) several MSS. exist; the second Greek version is much abbreviated; the Latin, on the other hand, is considerably enlarged. The two latter versions were discovered by Tischendorf, as also a third closely-related version, which he took to be a continuation of *Pseudo-Matthew*. The Syriac version of Dr. Wright is again short, and omits extensive portions. The character of the stories which make up the Gospel has already been described. The spirit which pervades them is well expressed in the remonstrance to Joseph of the parents whose child Jesus had killed: 'Since thou hast such a child, it is impossible for thee to live with us in the village; or else teach Him to bless and not to curse; for He is killing our children' (chap. iv.); and in the saying in chap. viii., 'And no one after that dared to make Him angry, lest He should curse him, and he should be maimed.' Only three or four miracles of mercy occur (chaps. vii., viii., xiv., xv.). In addition to the stories of miracles in the other versions, the Latin version has one of Jesus making a dried fish to breathe and swim.

I THOMAS, an Israelite,[1] write you this account, that all the brethren from among the heathen may know the miracles of our Lord Jesus Christ in His infancy,[2] which He did after His birth in our country. The beginning of it is as follows:—

Miracles of Jesus's Infancy

2. This child Jesus, when five years old,[3] was playing in the ford of a mountain stream; and He

---

[1] The Gospel professes to be written by 'Thomas the Israelite.' In the Latin version Thomas is identified with 'the Apostle of the Lord' (chap. iv.), and there is a second endorsement by him at the close. The work is really, as shown in the Introduction, of Gnostic origin.

[2] The special object of the Gospel is to recount the miracles of the infancy. The Latin version commences with three chapters relating to the sojourn in Egypt. These give one additional miracle, viz., the making a dried fish to live and swim (chap. i.). Chaps. xxvi. to xlii. of *Pseudo-Matthew* (*see* below) are simply another version of the Thomas-Gospel. They contain nearly all the miracles in the Greek and Syriac copies, with one or two additions.

[3] It may be convenient at this point to give a list of the miracles which form the staple of the Gospel. They are these, in order of the text:—

1. Jesus collects water into pools, and clears them (chap. ii.).
2. Challenged for breaking the Sabbath, He makes clay sparrows fly (chap. ii.).
3. Withers up the son of Annas, who had spoiled His pools (chap. iii.).
4. Kills a boy who jostles Him (chap. iv.).
5. Strikes His accusers with blindness (chap. v.).
6. Confounds the schoolmaster Zacchæus with His knowledge of the Hebrew letters (chaps. vi., vii.).
7. Heals those who had fallen under His curse (chap. viii.).

collected the flowing waters into pools, and made them clear immediately, and by a word alone He made them obey Him.[4] And having made some soft clay, He fashioned out of it twelve sparrows. And it was the Sabbath when He did these things. And there were also many other children playing with Him. And a certain Jew, seeing what Jesus was doing, playing on the Sabbath, went off immediately, and said to his father Joseph: Behold, thy son is at the stream, and has taken clay, and made of it twelve birds, and has profaned the Sabbath. And Joseph, coming to the place and seeing, cried out to Him, saying: Wherefore doest thou on the Sabbath what it is not lawful to do? And Jesus

---

8. Raises from the dead a boy fallen from a roof, whose death He had been accused of causing (chap. ix.).
9. Heals a youth's foot wounded by an axe (chap. x.).
10. Carries home water in His cloak—the pitcher being broken (chap. xi.).
11. Makes corn which He sows to multiply (chap. xii.).
12 Aids Joseph's carpentry by lengthening a piece of wood (chap. xiii.).
13. Kills a teacher who struck Him (chap. xiv.).
14. Preaches to another teacher, and restores the one He had killed (chap. xv.).
15. Cures James of a viper's bite, and kills the viper (chap. xvi.).
16. Gives life to a dead child (chap. xvii.).
17. Raises a dead man to life (chap. xviii.).

[4] Between the miracles of the pools and the making of the sparrows *Pseudo-Matthew* interpolates a duplicate of miracle No. 3, viz., the withering up of the boy who destroyed the pools. The story of the son of Annas, however, occurs in its own place.

clapped His hands, and cried out to the sparrows, and said to them: Off you go! And the sparrows flew, and went off crying. And the Jews seeing this were amazed, and went away and reported to their chief men what they had seen Jesus doing.

The Son of Annas withered up

3. And the son of Annas the scribe was standing there with Joseph; and he took a willow branch, and let out the waters which Jesus had collected. And Jesus, seeing what was done, was angry, and said to him: O wicked, impious, and foolish! what harm did the pools and the waters do to thee? Behold, even now thou shalt be dried up like a tree, and thou shalt not bring forth either leaves, or root, or fruit. And straightway that boy was quite dried up. And Jesus departed, and went to Joseph's house. But the parents of the boy that had been dried up took him up, bewailing his youth, and brought him to Joseph, and reproached him because [said they] thou hast such a child doing such things.

4. After that He was again passing through the village; and a boy ran up against Him,[5] and

---

[5] In the shorter Greek form the boy does not run against Jesus, but throws a stone at Him, and strikes His shoulder. The other versions give the story as in the text.

struck His shoulder. And Jesus was angry, and said to him: Thou shalt not go back the way thou camest. And immediately he fell down dead. And some who saw what had taken place, said: Whence was this child begotten, that every word of his is certainly accomplished? And the parents of the dead boy went away to Joseph, and blamed him, saying: Since thou hast such a child, it is impossible for thee to live with us in the village; or else teach him to bless, and not to curse: for he is killing our children.

Jesus admonished for inflicting Death on a Boy

5. And Joseph called the Child apart, and admonished Him, saying: Why doest thou such things, and these people suffer, and hate us, and persecute us? And Jesus said: I know that these words of thine are not thine own; nevertheless for thy sake I will be silent; but they shall bear their punishment. And straightway those that accused Him were struck blind. And those who saw it were much afraid and in great perplexity, and said about Him: Every word which he spoke, whether good or bad, was an act, and became a wonder. And when they saw that Jesus had done such a thing, Joseph rose and took hold of His ear, and pulled it hard. And the child was very angry, and said to him: It is enough for thee to

seek, and not to find;[6] and most certainly thou hast not done wisely. Knowest thou not that I am thine? Do not trouble me.

6. And a certain teacher, Zacchæus by name, was standing in a certain place, and heard Jesus thus speaking to his father; and he wondered exceedingly, that, being a child, he should speak in such a way. And a few days thereafter he came to Joseph, and said to him: Thou hast a sensible child, and he has some mind. Give him to me, then, that he may[7] learn letters; and I shall teach him along with the letters all knowledge, both how to address all the elders, and to honour them as forefathers and fathers, and how to love those of his own age. And He said to him all the letters from the Alpha even to the Omega, clearly and with great exactness. And He looked upon the teacher Zacchæus, and said to him: Thou who art ignorant of the nature of the Alpha, how canst thou teach others the Beta? Thou hypocrite! first, if thou knowest, teach the A, and

---

[6] Thilo interprets, with one of the MSS., 'It is enough for thee that they (the persons blinded) seek and are not able to find.' *Pseudo-Matthew* makes Jesus, at Joseph's remonstrance, take the dead boy by the ear and revive him (chap. xxix.).

[7] The story of Zacchæus and the Hebrew alphabet is a favourite one, and appears, but with variations, in all the versions. The similar story further down is only a variant of this. In *Pseudo-Matthew* Zacchæus does not himself teach the letters, but hands Jesus over to an old man, Master Levi, with whom the dialogue takes place (chap. xxxi.).

then we shall believe thee about the B. Then He began to question the teacher about the first letter, and he was not able to answer Him. And in the hearing of many, the child says to Zacchæus: Hear, O teacher, the order of the first letter,[8] and notice here how it has lines, and a middle stroke crossing those which thou seest common; (lines) brought together; the highest part supporting them, and again bringing them under one head; with three points [of intersection]; of the same kind; principal and subordinate; of equal length. Thou hast the lines of the A.

Zacchæus essays to teach Jesus

7. And when the teacher Zacchæus[9] heard the child speaking such and so great allegories of the first letter, he was at a great loss about such a narrative, and about His teaching. And he said to those that were present: Alas! I, wretch that I am, am at a loss, bringing shame upon myself by having dragged this child hither. Take him away,

---

[8] The passage on the mysteries of the letter Alpha is hopelessly corrupt, and is unintelligible. The form of letter that best answers to the description is the old Phœnician 'A,' which somewhat resembles the letter 'V' laid sidewise, with a cross-intersecting stroke.

[9] One MS., after a brief allusion to Zacchæus going home ashamed, substitutes for chap. vii. a fragment of the story of the changing of the colours of cloth in the dyer's shop, as given in the *Arabic Gospel of the Infancy*, chap. xxxvii.

then, I beseech thee, brother Joseph. I cannot endure the sternness of his look; I cannot make out his meaning at all. That child does not belong to this earth; he can tame even fire. Assuredly he was born before the creation of the world.[10] What sort of a belly bore him, what sort of a womb nourished him, I do not know. Alas! my friend, he has carried me away; I cannot get at his meaning: thrice wretched that I am, I have deceived myself. I made a struggle to have a scholar, and I was found to have a teacher. My mind is filled with shame, my friends, because I, an old man, have been conquered by a child. There is nothing for me but despondency and death on account of this boy, for I am not able at this hour to look him in the face; and when everybody says that I have been beaten by a little child, what can I say? And how can I give an account of the lines of the first letter that he spoke about? I know not, O my friends; for I can make neither beginning nor end of him. Therefore, I beseech thee, brother Joseph, take

---

[10] 'Born before the creation of the world.' The shorter Greek Gospel makes Jesus say to Zacchæus, 'I know more than you, for I am before the ages.... Assuredly I know when the world was created' (chap. vi.). Similarly in *Pseudo-Matthew*, 'I have seen Abraham, whom you call your father, and have spoken with him; and he has seen me' (chap. xxx.).

him home. What great thing he is, either god or angel, or what I am to say, I know not.

Zacchæus put to Shame

8. And when the Jews were encouraging Zacchæsus, the child laughed aloud, and said: Now let thy learning bring forth fruit, and let the blind in heart see. I am here from above, that I may curse them, and call them to the things that are above, as He that sent me on your account has commanded me. And when the child ceased speaking, immediately all were made whole who had fallen under His curse. And no one after that dared to make Him angry, lest he should curse him, and he should be maimed.

Zeno and a Young Man brought to Life

9. And some days after, Jesus was playing in an upper room of a certain house, and one of the children that were playing with Him fell down from the house, and was killed. And, when the other children saw this, they ran away, and Jesus alone stood still. And the parents of the dead child coming, reproached Jesus, and they threatened Him. And Jesus leaped down from the roof, and stood beside the body of the child, and cried with a loud voice, and said: Zeno—for that was his name—stand up, and tell me; did I throw thee down? And he stood up immediately,

and said: Certainly not, my lord; thou didst not throw me down, but hast raised me up. And those that saw this were struck with astonishment. And the child's parents glorified God on account of the miracle that had happened, and adored Jesus.

10. A few days after, a young man was splitting wood in the corner, and the axe came down and cut the sole of his foot in two, and he died from loss of blood. And there was a great commotion, and people ran together, and the child Jesus ran there too. And he pressed through the crowd, and laid hold of the young man's wounded foot, and he was cured immediately. And He said to the young man: Rise up now, split the wood, and remember me. And the crowd seeing what had happened, adored the child, saying: Truly the Spirit of God dwells in this child.

Sundry Miracles

11. And when He was six years old, His mother gave Him a pitcher, and sent Him to draw water, and bring it into the house. But He struck against some one in the crowd, and the pitcher was broken. And Jesus unfolded the cloak which He had on, and filled it with water, and carried it to His mother. And His mother, seeing the miracle that had happened, kissed

Him, and kept within herself the mysteries which she had seen Him doing.

12. And again in seed-time the child went out with His father to sow corn in their land. And while His father was sowing, the child Jesus also sowed one grain of corn. And when He had reaped it, and threshed it, He made a hundred kors;[11] and calling all the poor of the village to the threshing-floor, He gave them the corn, and Joseph took away what was left of the corn. And He was eight years old when He did this miracle.

13. And His father was a carpenter, and at that time made ploughs and yokes. And a certain rich man ordered him to make him a couch. And one of what is called the cross pieces being too short, they did not know what to do. The child Jesus[12] said to His father Joseph: Put down the two pieces of wood, and make them even in the middle. And Joseph did as the child said to him. And Jesus stood at the other end, and took hold of the shorter piece of wood, and stretched it, and made it equal to the other. And His father Joseph saw it, and wondered, and embraced the

---

[11] 'Kor'=homer. Jerome states that the kor equals 30 *modii*. Jahn reckons it at 32 pecks, I pint.

[12] Justin Martyr says that Jesus, working as a carpenter, 'made ploughs and yokes' (*Dial.* 88), which may be an allusion to this passage.

child, and kissed Him, saying: Blessed am I, because God has given me this child.

Jesus's Second Teacher

14. And Joseph, seeing that the child was vigorous in mind and body, again resolved that He should not remain ignorant of the letters, and took Him away, and handed Him over to another teacher. And the teacher said to Joseph:[13] I shall first teach him the Greek letters, and then the Hebrew. For the teacher was aware of the trial that had been made of the child, and was afraid of Him. Nevertheless he wrote out the alphabet, and gave Him all his attention for a long time, and He made him no answer. And Jesus said to him: If thou art really a teacher, and art well acquainted with the letters, tell me the power of the Alpha, and I will tell thee the power of the Beta. And the teacher was enraged at this, and struck Him on the head. And the child, being in pain, cursed him; and immediately he swooned away, and fell to the ground on his face. And the child returned to Joseph's house; and Joseph was grieved, and gave orders to His mother, saying: Do not let him go outside of the door, because those that make him angry die.

---

[13] Evidently a duplicate of the story of Zacchæus. It is referred to by Irenæus (i. 20).

15. And after some time, another master again, a genuine friend of Joseph, said to him: Bring the child to my school; perhaps I shall be able to flatter him into learning his letters. And Joseph said: If thou hast the courage, brother, take him with thee. And he took Him with him in fear and great agony; but the child went along pleasantly. And going boldly into the school, He found a book lying on the reading-desk; and taking it, He read not the letters that were in it, but opening His mouth, He spoke by the Holy Spirit, and taught the law to those that were standing round. And a great crowd having come together, stood by and heard Him, and wondered at the ripeness of His teaching, and the readiness of His words, and that He, child as He was, spoke in such a way. And Joseph hearing of it, was afraid, and ran to the school, in doubt lest this master too should be without experience. And the master said to Joseph: Know, brother, that I have taken the child as a scholar, and he is full of much grace and wisdom; but I beseech thee, brother, take him home. And when the child heard this, He laughed at him directly, and said: Since thou hast spoken aright, and witnessed aright, for thy sake he also that was struck down shall be cured. And immediately the other master was cured. And Joseph took the child, and went away home.

Jesus's Third Teacher

16. And Joseph sent his son James to tie up wood and bring it home, and the child Jesus also followed him. And when James was gathering the fagots, a viper bit James' hand. And when he was racked [with pain], and at the point of death, Jesus came near and blew upon the bite; and the pain ceased directly, and the beast burst, and instantly James remained safe and sound.

Other Miracles of raising the Dead

17. And after this the infant of one of Joseph's neighbours fell sick and died, and its mother wept sore. And Jesus heard that there was great lamentation and commotion, and ran in haste, and found the child dead, and touched his breast, and said: I say to thee, child, be not dead, but live, and be with thy mother. And directly it looked up and laughed. And he said to the woman: Take it, and give it milk, and remember me. And seeing this, the crowd that was standing by wondered, and said: Truly this child was either God or an angel of God, for every word of his is a certain fact. And Jesus went out thence, playing with the other children.

18. And some time after there occurred a great commotion while a house was building, and Jesus stood up and went away to the place.

And seeing a man lying dead, He took him by the hand, and said:[14] Man, I say to thee, arise, and go on with thy work. And directly he rose up, and adored Him. And seeing this, the crowd wondered, and said: This child is from heaven,[15] for he has saved many souls from death, and he continues to save during all his life.

Jesus and the Doctors

19. And when He was twelve years old His[16] parents went as usual to Jerusalem to the feast of the passover with their fellow-travellers. And after the passover they were coming home again. And while they were coming home, the child Jesus went back to Jerusalem. And His parents thought that he was in the company. And having gone one day's journey, they sought for Him among their relations; and not finding Him, they were in great grief, and turned back to the city seeking for Him. And after the third day they found Him in the temple, sitting in the midst of the teachers, both hearing the law and asking them questions. And they were all attending to Him, and wondering that He, being a child, was

---

[14] This story of the raising of the workman is wanting in *Pseudo-Matthew*, but instead of it is a story of the raising of a rich man from the dead at Capernaum (chap. xl.).

[15] The spirit of mercy here ascribed to Jesus is certainly not predominant in the Gospel.

[16] This narrative, of course, is based on Luke 2:41–52.

shutting the mouths of the elders and teachers of the people, explaining the main points of the law and the parables of the prophets. And his mother Mary coming up, said to Him: Why hast thou done this to us, child? Behold, we have been seeking for thee in great trouble. And Jesus said to them: Why do you seek me? Do you not know that I must be about my Father's business? And the scribes and the Pharisees said: Art thou the mother of this child? And she said: I am. And they said to her: Blessed art thou among women, for God hath blessed the fruit of thy womb; for such glory, and such virtue and wisdom, we have neither seen nor heard ever. And Jesus rose up, and followed His mother, and was subject to His parents. And His mother observed all these things that had happened. And Jesus advanced in wisdom, and stature, and grace. To whom be glory for ever and ever. Amen.

About CrossReach Publications

Thank you for choosing CrossReach Publications.

Our philosophy is to remain as neutral as possible. We are non-denominational and non-sectarian. We seek to publish books from a wide variety of authors and doctrinal positions, on a wide variety of Christian topics that will teach, encourage, challenge, inspire and equip. We appreciate and respect what every part of the body brings to the table and believe everyone has the right to study and come to their own conclusions. *We aim to help to facilitate that end.*

We aspire to excellence. If we have not met your standards please contact us and let us know. We want you to feel satisfied with your product. Amy, our 11 year old, has recently joined the business now and is publishing her own books. And Sarah, our 5 year old, loves to mimic daddy "doing the books"!
We're a family-based home-business. A husband and wife team raising 8 kids. You can see us in action in our family vlog. If you have any questions or comments about our publications or our channel you can do so by emailing us.

www.YouTube.com/c/TheKinsellaBunchVlog
CrossReach@outlook.com

Don't forget you can follow us on Facebook and Twitter, and keep up to date on our newest releases and deals.

More Apocrypha & Pseudepigrapha Titles

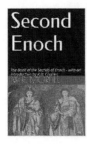

Second Enoch
W. R. Morfil

Includes an introduction by R.H. Charles, famed translator of the 1st Book of Enoch. This book makes up part of what is now known as the Old Testament Pseudepigrapha. It will be of major interest to students of ancient religion, Judaism, early Christianity and more.

The Epistle of Polycarp to the Philippians and the Martyrdom of Polycarp
J. B. Lightfoot

THE Epistle is usually made a sort of preface to those of Ignatius, for reasons which will be obvious to the reader. Yet he was born later, and lived to a much later period. They seem to have been friends from the days of their common pupilage under St. John; and there is nothing improbable in the conjecture of Usher, that he was the "angel of the church in Smyrna," to whom the Master says, "Be thou faithful unto death, and I will give thee a crown of life." His pupil Irenaeus gives us one of the very few portraits of an apostolic man which are to be found in antiquity, in a few sentences which are a picture: "I could describe the very place in which the blessed Polycarp sat and taught; his going out and coming in; the whole tenor of his life; his personal appearance; how he would speak of the conversations he had held with John and with others who had seen the Lord. How did he make mention of their words and of whatever he had heard from them respecting the Lord." Thus he unconsciously tantalizes our reverent curiosity. Alas! that such conversations were not written for our learning. But there is a wise Providence in what is withheld, as well as in the inestimable treasures we have received.

THE Martyrdom purports to have been written by the church at Smyrna to the church at Philomelium, and through that church to the whole Christian world, in order to give a succinct account of the circumstances attending the martyrdom of Polycarp. It is the earliest of all the Martyria, and has generally been accounted both the most interesting and authentic. Not a few, however, deem it interpolated in several passages, and some refer it to a much later date than the middle of the second century, to which it has been commonly ascribed. We cannot tell how much it may owe to the writers who successively transcribed it. Great part of it has been engrossed by Eusebius in his Ecclesiastical History (iv. 15); and it is instructive to observe, that some of the most startling miraculous phenomena recorded in the text as it now stands, have no place in the narrative as given by that early historian of the church. Much discussion has arisen respecting several particulars contained in this Martyrium; but into these disputes we do not enter, having it for our aim simply to present the reader with as faithful a translation as possible of this very interesting monument of Christian antiquity.

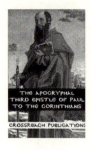

The Apocryphal Third Epistle of Paul to the Corinthians: or 3 Corinthians
M. R. James

This epistle, often considered one of the forgotten, forbidden or lost books of the Bible is purported to be the third of three letters to the Corinthians by the Apostle Paul. While the canonical epistles are regarded almost unanimously as genuine writings of the renowned New Testament writer, this writing is universally rejected as pseudepigraphal. In saying that it was accepted as canonical in some parts of the East at various times during the middle ages.

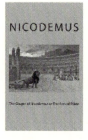

The Gospel of Nicodemus or The Acts of Pilate

Although this Gospel is, by some among the learned, supposed to have been really written by Nicodemus, who became a disciple of Jesus Christ, and conversed with him; others conjecture that it was a forgery towards the close of the third century by some zealous believer, who observing that there had been appeals made by the Christians of the former age, to the Acts of Pilate, but that such Acts could not be produced, imagined it would be of service to Christianity to fabricate and publish this Gospel; as it would both confirm the Christians under persecution, and convince the Heathens of the truth of the Christian religion. The Rev. Jeremiah Jones says, that such pious frauds were very common among Christians even in the first three centuries; and that a forgery of this nature, with the view above mentioned, seems natural and probable. The same author, in noticing that Eusebius, in his Ecclesiastical history, charges the Pagans with having forged and published a book, called "The Acts of Pilate," takes occasion to observe, that the internal evidence of this Gospel shows it was not the work of any Heathen; but that if in the latter end of the third century we find it in use among Christians (as it was then certainly in some churches) and about the same time find a forgery of the Heathens under the same title, it seems exceedingly probable that some Christians, at that time, should publish such a piece as this, in order partly to confront the spurious one of the Pagans, and partly to support those appeals which had been made by former Christians to the Acts of Pilate; and Mr. Jones says, he thinks so more particularly as we have innumerable instances of forgeries by the faithful in the primitive ages, grounded on less plausible reasons. Whether it be canonical or not, it is of very great antiquity, and is appealed to by several of the ancient Christians.

The Shepherd of Hermas
J. B. Lightfoot

The Shepherd of Hermas is an astounding piece of ancient Christian writing. It is usually dated at between 120 Ad and 150 Ad. This means that the author may have been in contact with an Apostle such as John who died around 98 Ad. And he was most certainly contemporaneous with those who knew some of the Apostle such as Ignatius and Polycarp.

Psalms of Solomon & Odes of Solomon
James Rendel Harris & R. H. Charles

In the Odes we have few quotations or adaptations from previous writings, whether Jewish or Christian; there is little that can be traced to the Old Testament, almost nothing that is to be credited to the Gospels or other branches of the Christian literature. Their radiance is no reflection from the illumination of other days: their inspiration is first-hand and immediate; it answers very well to the summary which Aristides made of the life of the early Christian Church when he described them as indeed 'a new people with whom something Divine is mingled.' They are thus altogether distinct from the extant Psalms of Solomon.

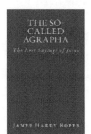

The So-Called Agrapha: The Lost Sayings of Jesus
James Hardy Ropes

To know a little more of the life of Christ, whether of his works or words, than the tradition embodied in the gospels tells has from early times been the eager desire of men. Apocryphal books almost without number have one after another held the attention of great numbers of Christians, only to be recognized in the end as disappointing fictions. One line of serious investigation, however, has been followed persistently and hopefully— the search for scattered sayings of the Lord preserved outside of the canonical gospels, the so-called Agrapha. One of these is familar to all, the word quoted in Paul's speech at Miletus, Acts 20:35, and was early noticed. That the writings of the Fathers contain others which may have claims to genuineness was also seen centuries ago, and the great patristic editors of the seventeenth and eighteenth centuries collected in their notes much valuable material bearing on the subject. Collections of the sayings themselves were also made, and under various names (among which that of "Agrapha" seems first to occur in 1776) have been current ever since Grabe published in 1698 in his Spicilegium eleven Dicta Jesu Christi quæ in IV. Evangeliis non extant. Of recent collections of the more important Agrapha, R. Hofmann's, in his Leben Jesu nach den Apokryphen, Westcott's, in his Introduction to the Study of the Gospels, and Schaff's, in the first volume of his History of the Christian Church, are easily accessible and convenient examples. These and similar collections have generally contained from twenty to thirty sayings, and have been largely dependent on the lists of Grabe and Fabricius.

The 400 Silent Years: from Malachi to Matthew
H. A. Ironside

Fully illustrated. Includes all of the drawings from the original edition. What is the history between the Old and New Testaments? Most people are not even aware there is such a gap. But there is. A 400 year gap. When the Old Testament leaves off the Jews have just returned back from Babylonian captivity and the Persian Empire is in full swing. When Jesus enters the scene it is 400 years later. The Persians are long gone, the Greeks have had their time and now the Romans rule to roost. So what happened? Do we have any writings from this time? Could understanding this period of time help us understand the New Testament, the world of Jesus and the Apostles? The answer is yes. This exciting book by well-known author H. A. Ironside lifts the veil from this vital period of Jewish history and helps piece together the events that brought them from Malachi to Matthew. This book will be of interest to students of Biblical, Ancient Near Eastern, Greek and Roman history as well as all those who desire to know and understand the Bible for fully.

The Epistle of Barnabas
Kirsopp Lake

The document which is always known as the Epistle of Barnabas is, like 1st Clement, really anonymous, and it is generally regarded as impossible to accept the tradition which ascribes it to the Barnabas who was a companion of S. Paul, though it is convenient to continue to use the title.

It is either a general treatise or was intended for some community in which Alexandrian ideas prevailed, though it is not possible to define either its destination, or the locality from which it was written, with any greater accuracy. Its main object is to warn Christians against a Judaistic conception of the Old Testament, and the writer carries a symbolic exegesis as far as did Philo; indeed he goes farther and apparently denies any literal significance at all to the commands of the Law. The literal exegesis of the ceremonial law is to him a device of an evil angel who deceived the Jews.

The Epistle of Barnabas
Charles H. Hoole

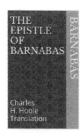

We owe to the discovery of the Codex Sinaiticus the Greek text of the epistle of St. Barnabas.1 In that manuscript it comes at the end of the New Testament, between the Book of Revelation and the Shepherd of Hernias, with which the manuscript concludes, The heading is simply the Epistle of Barnabas, and the title is repeated at the end. Previous to the discovery of this manuscript, though a considerable portion of the Greek remained, chapters 1-4 were lost, and the epistle was known chiefly by an ancient Latin version, which is itself imperfect, the three concluding chapters being lost; the portion which remained in Greek furnished only a very inferior text, and the epistle could not consequently be read in a state which would assure us that we had the work in the same shape as it presented in the Ante-Nicene period.

We have a large selection of Evangelical titles
All available on the Amazon and Createspace stores
Just search for CrossReach Publications!

Made in United States
Troutdale, OR
06/18/2024